Canada's Titanic: The History and Legacy of the RMS *Empress of Ireland*

By Charles River Editors

About Charles River Editors

Charles River Editors is a boutique digital publishing company, specializing in bringing history back to life with educational and engaging books on a wide range of topics. Keep up to date with our new and free offerings with this 5 second sign up on our weekly mailing list, and visit Our Kindle Author Page to see other recently published Kindle titles.

We make these books for you and always want to know our readers' opinions, so we encourage you to leave reviews and look forward to publishing new and exciting titles each week.

Introduction

G. Bouchard's picture of a memorial at Pointe-au-Père

The RMS *Empress of Ireland*

"A blow, a ripping, the side taken out of a ship, darkness, the inrush of waters, a panic, and then in the hush the silent corpses drifting by. So with the Canadian liner. She has gone to her grave leaving a trail of sorrow behind her. Hundreds of human hearts and homes are in mourning for the loss of dear companions and friends." – Logan Marshall, *The tragic story of the Empress of Ireland*

There is something romantic about traveling on a cruise ship, and even today, luxury cruises are considered by many to be the ultimate vacation, featuring days of fun activities in exotic locations and nights of dinner and dancing under the stars. Today even the cheapest cabins are quite luxurious, and people save for years to afford to travel by sea.

However, it was not always that way, and there was a time when travelling on even the most luxurious liners could prove dangerous or even deadly. The loss of the Titanic in 1912 cast a pall over all future voyages, and in the wake of the most famous sinking in history, a number of crucial changes were made, including the requirement that there be enough lifeboats available for every passenger, a change that was codified by the International Convention for the Safety of Life at Sea in 1914.

That same convention also made a change to the way distress signals were used, and the British subsequently ensured that the bulkheads be raised higher up the boat to truly ensure that the compartments were watertight. Gone were the days that safety would be compromised for the comforts of the First Class. And of course, a bunch of changes were made to the way ships navigated around icebergs.

In the wake of the Titanic, people tried to assure each other that a similar disaster could never happen again, but it did just two years later on a chilly night in 1914. This time, it was not an iceberg that did the damage but another vessel that sent the *Empress of Ireland* to her watery grave. Likewise, her passengers did not perish in the frigid Atlantic but along the banks of the St. Lawrence River in Canada. As Logan Marshall lamented, "'Those who go down to the sea in ships' was once a synonym for those who gambled with death and put their lives upon the hazard. Today the mortality at sea is less than on common carriers on land. But the futility of absolute prevention of accident is emphasized again and again. The regulation of safety makes catastrophes like that of the *Empress of Ireland* all the more tragic and terrible."

Though the tale of the ship's fate pales in comparison to that of the Titanic, the loss of life in 1914 was nearly as great as it was in 1912. Indeed, with the Titanic's massive shadow all but obscuring the *Empress of Ireland*, the 1914 disaster remains one of the great little-known tragedies of the 20th century, and to this day in Canada, Canadians refer to it as "Canada's Titanic."

Canada's Titanic: The History and Legacy of the RMS Empress of Ireland examines one of the 20th century's largest maritime tragedies, and the worst in Canadian history. Along with pictures of important people, places, and events, you will learn about the RMS *Empress of Ireland* like never before, in no time at all.

The Start of the Fateful Voyage

"Science has wrought miracles for the greater protection of those afloat. Wireless telegraphy, air-tight compartments, the construction which has produced what is called 'the unsinkable ship' have added greatly to the safety of ocean travel. But science cannot eliminate the element of error." – Logan Marshall

In 1907, Europe and the United States were enjoying a time of peace and prosperity that had not seen for more than 40 years and would not be seen again for another 40. England had finally made peace with most of her enemies, even if that peace was sometimes uneasy, and she was even experiencing something of an internal peace, for while the difficulties with Ireland continued, they were at least further under the surface than they had been in the past. Queen Victoria's much beloved son, the popular King Edward VII, was on the throne, and along with his wife, Queen Alexandria, the Royal Family did an excellent job of presenting a formidable and cheerful face to the country. Likewise, all was well in the United States, which had finally recovered from the aftermath of the Civil War and had a sense of stability and security.

As is often the case, tranquility fosters prosperity, and businessmen on both sides of the Atlantic were finding ways to use all the new technologies available to improve the lives of others while lining their own pockets. In addition to all the new small appliances being made available, there had also been major strides made when it came to large-scale construction, so it had become both faster and easier to build even such giant edifices as skyscrapers and large ships.

Large ships were particularly lucrative for two reasons. On the one hand, the nouveau rich enjoyed nothing as much as a transatlantic voyage, and they also expected all the most luxurious accommodations and latest amenities on those ships. At the same time, even those who were not incredibly wealthy knew that sailing was the only way to get from one side of the globe to the other, so the monolithic giants being built in Europe and America during this era were not just for the rich. The companies that owned these liners knew that the poor also wanted to be able to travel, particularly as immigrants to the United States, and that these people would willingly part with their life savings for a small berth in the crowded steerage portions of the ships. Though they would only catch glimpses of those who lived in luxury above them, the immigrants sailing to America were happy to get there just the same.

Given the money to be made, there was a strong sense of competition among the major shipping companies, and many of the new state of the art ships were made in the British Isles. According to an article appearing in the *Boston Globe* just after the accident, "The *Empress of Ireland* was built in Glasgow. She is 570 feet in length and 63 feet 6 inches beam. Her registered tonnage is 14,500 and her displacement about 20,000. She has accommodations for 350 first class passengers, 350 second class and 1000 steerage." Another *Globe* article added, "With her sister boats both on the east coast and on the west, the *Empress of Ireland* was part of the 'all

Red Line' which carried the imperial mails from Liverpool to Hong Kong. There are five passenger decks and the boat deck above them constitute a promenade a fifth of a mile in length."

In fact, the ship, designed by Francis Elgar, had been built in Glasgow and launched in 1906. She typically carried a crew of just under 400 and could comfortably accommodate more than 1,500 passengers. First Class included a number of suites and a Café, as well as Music and Smoking Rooms and a Library. The large dining room featured an impressive domed ceiling. Second Class was also quite comfortable, and even steerage was improved, with more mature passengers and families being able to opt for the more comfortable Third Class while single men and women, and those with only the smallest of means, could still afford basic accommodations in Fourth Class.

Elgar

A contemporary sketch of the RMS *Empress of Ireland*

The passengers and crew who boarded the *Empress* on the morning of May 28, 1914 were anticipating nothing special in their voyage. For most, this was not a vacation trip but a convenient and comfortable means of getting from Quebec City to Liverpool. That said, they might have been concerned had they known that this was the captain's maiden voyage down the St. Lawrence River. In fact, Henry George Kendall had only been captain of the vessel for less than a month, and though he had sailed on the St. Lawrence before, he had never commanded a vessel of such size down the often treacherous river.

Kendall

The ship left from Quebec City at 4:30 that fateful afternoon and sailed all night, reaching Father Point, near Rimouski, in the wee hours of the following morning. After a brief stay there, the ship was on her way again, and while it wouldn't get far, the passengers had no way of knowing that. As Marshall Logan noted in his work about the sinking, the mood on board during the first night was festive: "Twilight settled without dampening the gay humor of the throng. The first meal on board was eaten with a relish which only the occasion could impart, and the passengers disposed themselves for the full enjoyment of the evening."

The Collision and Sinking

"In a moment the fate of the Empress was known to all. The one smashing blow had done for her and the great bull-nose of the 3,500-ton freighter had crashed through the ribs and bulkheads. The one pithy sentence of Captain Kendall summed all. 'The ship is gone,' he said; 'women to the boats.'" – Logan Marshall

At about 2:00 a.m. on the morning of May 29, the SS *Storstad*, a Norwegian collier, slammed into the *Empress*, ripping a hole in her starboard side that ultimately capsized the ship and sent it to the bottom in just 15 minutes. No one could ever agree on exactly how the accident occurred, but the two men who could best explain what happened were the men captaining the two ships.

A picture of the *Storstad* in Montreal after the collision

A picture of the damage

In the ensuing investigation, Captain Kendall insisted that it was the fault of the *Storstad's* captain, Thomas Anderson. Kendall testified, "The Storstad was then about one point on my starboard bow. At that time I saw a slight fog bank coming gradually from the land and knew it was going to pass between the Storstad and myself. The Storstad was about two miles away at the time. Then the fog came and the Storstad lights disappeared. I rang full speed astern on my engines and stopped my ship. At the same time I blew three short blasts on the steamer's whistle, meaning ' I am going full speed astern.'"

Kendall testified that the other ship must have heard him based on the response: "The Storstad answered with the whistle, giving me one prolonged blast. I then looked over the side of my ship into the water and saw my ship was stopped. I stopped my engines and blew two long blasts, meaning ' my ship was under way but stopped and has no way upon her. He answered me again with one prolonged blast. The sound was then about four points upon my starboard bow. It was still foggy. I then looked out to where the sound came from."

By the time Kendall next caught sight of the other vessel, it was too late to prevent a disaster: "About two minutes afterward I saw his red and green lights. He would then be about one ship's length away from me. I shouted to him through the megaphone to go full speed astern as I saw the danger of collision was inevitable. At the same time I put my engines full speed ahead, with my helm hard aport, with the object of avoiding, if possible, the shock. Almost at the same time he came right in and cut me down in a line between the funnels."

Not surprisingly, Captain Thomas Anderson told a somewhat different story, claiming that "the vessels sighted each other when far apart. The *Empress of Ireland* was seen off the port bow of the Storstad. The *Empress of Ireland*'s green or starboard light was visible to those on the Storstad. Under these circumstances the rules of navigation gave the Storstad the right of way. The heading of the Empress was then changed in such a manner as to put the vessels in a position to pass safely. Shortly after a fog enveloped first the Empress and then the Storstad...Fog signals were exchanged. The Storstad's engines were at once slowed and then stopped. Her heading remained unaltered. Whistles from the Empress were heard on the Storstad's port bow and were answered. The *Empress of Ireland* was then seen through the fog close at hand on the port bow of the Storstad. She was showing her green light and was making considerable headway. The engines of the Storstad were at once reversed at full speed and her headway was nearly checked when the vessels came together."

Anderson

Passenger John Fowler became an important witness during the investigation of the event because he was one of the few who actually saw the collision. When asked about the fog, he said "there was fog, but it was not very thick," adding that he heard the *Empress'* siren blaring before the collision. "I heard the siren blowing a great deal, and got up to look out to see whether we were passing another vessel or were whistling for a pilot. I had just got my head out through the hole when the collier drove right into us just beyond me. And then we gradually went over to one side."

Still not realizing the desperate nature of the situation, Fowler recounted what happened next: "I tried to quiet the people when I got out by telling them that it was all right, and that the boat would right herself. I saw a lady with two children, a small baby and one little girl of six, and I put on them a lifebelt each, which I grabbed from the spare ones by the side of the stairs. I took them on deck and in a kind of panic we lost each other and I don't know if any of them were saved...I climbed up to the second saloon deck and went along there and saw Miss Wilmot struggling to get up the steps. She could not do so, as the boat was listing so badly and there was a lot of water in the passage, into which she fell back. The ship was so much to one side that you could walk on her plates as on a floor."

Regardless of which account of the collision, if any, was completely accurate, the result was tragically chaotic all the same. Logan Marshall described the pandemonium on the stricken ship: "Instantly, it seemed as though there was a nightmare of sounds, cries of fear and agony that were too awful to be real. All lights went out almost at once. More than 1,400 persons were fighting for life in the black dark; yet, for the most part the flight was not one of panic, but grim determination to find, if possible, some means of safety…"

Meanwhile, Marshall explained some of the ways the crew leapt into action in an effort to contain and minimize the damage, albeit futilely: "Kendall was hurt and in great pain, but he showed the pluck and decision of a naval officer. In the first minute of the disaster he ordered young Edward Bomford, the wireless operator, to flash the S. O. S. call, the cry for help that every ship must heed. He ordered officers and stewards to collect as many passengers as could be found and hold them for the boats. He had nine life-boats overboard within ten minutes. The S. O. S. call was ticked out by Edward Bomford, the junior wireless operator. Bomford had just come on duty to relieve Ronald Ferguson, when the Storstad rammed the Empress. Both young men were thrown to the deck. As they picked themselves up they heard the chorus of the disaster, the cries, groans and screams of injured and drowning passengers. An officer came running to the wireless house with orders from Captain Kendall, but Bomford, at the key, didn't have to wait for orders. He began to call the Marconi station at Father Point, and kept at it desperately until he had the ear of the Father Point operator."

Over 1,000 of the more than 1,400 aboard would lose their lives and never be able to tell their stories, but the few who survived later shared with the world descriptions of those harrowing 15 minutes. One man recalled, "I was asleep like most of the passengers when the collision came. There was a sickening crunching of wood and steel and then a grinding, ripping sound as the Storstad smashed her way along the port side of our ship. I knew that we had been struck and I rushed to the staterooms of some friends and shouted to them to get up, as the ship was sinking. Stateroom doors flew open all along the corridor and men and women began to rush for the grand companion forward. On deck officers of the ship, partially dressed, were rushing about urging passengers to be calm. Sailors under orders were trying to launch be lifeboats."

As he also pointed out, making it to the upper decks in no way guaranteed safety: "The darkness was intense and a few minutes after I reached the deck the electric lights went out. At that time there were still hundreds of passengers below trying to grope their way through the darkened corridors to the companion way and reach the deck. Most of them went down with the ship, for the corridors below filled right after the explosion of the boilers. I leaped overboard in despair just before the ship went down and managed to find a bit of wreckage to which I clung."

The biggest factor in the size and scope of the disaster was just how quickly the ship went down. Another survivor explained, "The collier, being only something over 3,000 tons, did not reach up even to the upper or topmost deck of our hull. Her bow cut under the upper deck and took a peeling off the side of our ship that allowed the water to rush into the lower deck B. Then the liner heeled over, and even those in the superstructure deck rooms had no chance to save themselves. Hundreds of them must have been dumped out of their berths and slammed against the walls with stunning force."

Staff Captain McCameron was one of more than 140 members of the Toronto's Salvation Army present on the ship that terrible night, and he subsequently spoke eloquently of his own fight for survival: "What an unspeakable confusion there was on the listing decks! With every lurch of the steamer we had to take a step higher and higher to the upper side, and finally I gained the rail, and stuck to it. I could swim, but I knew the mad folly of jumping into that swirling cataract at the side of the ship. She was sinking, inch by inch, now faster and faster. In a breathless moment, I felt the last rush to the bottom. A moment we hung on the surface."

After what seemed like an eternity, McCameron and the other on board felt what he described as "an endless, dreadful force [dragging] us down…How deep I went I cannot know, of course. It was yards and yards. Then came the cresting of the wave, and I was buoyed up on it. I had clutched tight at my senses meanwhile, and strove not to lose my head. The moment my head emerged, I saw a dark object on the water. I struck out for this, and soon was grasping the keel of an overturned ship's boat. I clambered aboard, not much the worse, and not very unduly excited."

McCameron was not alone on his little boat for very long: "Three or four more men also managed to get on the rocking back of the boat, and we then got to another which we righted, and got into. The canvas covering had not been taken from this boat, and a member of the crew, who was of us, ripped this open and enabled us to board it. The oars were intact. Within a few minutes, therefore, we were at work rescuing the people whose bodies eddied about us in circles."

Thus it was that a man typically more dedicated to saving souls spent the next critical moments of his life saving lives. One man almost made in on board, only to grow weak and slip away. They were able to rescue a woman, and McCameron recalled that the ship's surgeon "saved dozens of lives by his work of resuscitation on land. No sooner had we got to shore, than he had us at work manipulating the chests and limbs of the apparently drowned in efforts to save them. He was a Heaven-sent messenger to many stricken souls."

It's altogether possible if not likely that every passenger's mind immediately conjured up the harrowing tales they had heard or read about the loss of the *Titanic* just two years earlier. The influence of the *Titanic* was apparent in the reminiscences of another member of the Salvation Army, Miss Alice Bales: "I thought we had struck an iceberg when I heard the fearful grinding in the bows. With a cry to the girls who were with me, I stumbled out of the narrow stateroom, and groped up to the deck. Here was chaos. The ship was listing, listing, listing. Every step I took to the uppermost part of the deck, I seemed to be slipping back into that maelstrom of water and falling bodies. Finally, I gained the rail."

Unlike McCameron, Bales chose to take her chances in the water: "I climbed up on the rail, and with a prayer in my heart I jumped into the blackness. The water surged over my head. Down, down, I went. I could not swim a stroke. But I remembered that you should keep the air in your lungs, and as I sank I clenched my jaws, determined to stay with the battle as long as strength lasted. After long, long periods of struggle and fainting and renewed struggle, I saw a man, not far off, swimming with a life-belt. I forgot to tell you that I fastened a belt around my waist when I jumped."

Bales was eventually able to get a hold of the man's belt, and he began to give her a crash course in swimming. "I used every fibre and nerve to make the motions. I knew this was the chance for life. Then, when my energy was going fast, I heard a faint cry. There was a cluster of people. It was a life-boat. ... Someone was lifting me, dragging me over something hard. Now they were speaking to me. They revived me, and I was got aboard the Storstad, the ship that struck us."

When the collision occurred, another member of the Salvation Army, Major Atwell, was further from the point of contact than McCameron and Bales. In fact, he was far enough away that he claimed he "had an idea at the time that we had perhaps struck the tender, so slight appeared the shock. I did not look upon it as anything serious, but my wife thought I had better get up. My wife and I went on deck and we found that the vessel was listing and the list was increasing. [Soon] It was so great that I could see no chance of getting into a life-boat, even if one was launched, and I did not see how one could be launched."

At that point, Atwell knew he had to act fast. "So I fastened a life-belt round my wife and put one on myself. As the vessel heeled over, we clung to the rail and finally clambered over it on the side of the ship. As the boat sank, we clambered farther and farther along the side in the direction of the keel, until we had climbed, I think, a third of the way. Finally we jumped into the water and were picked up by one of the life-boats."

Mrs. Atwell also described the experience: "I was just lightly sleeping when I heard a slight crash. ...Then I heard the engines start, going as hard as they could. ...we got up almost directly, but by that time the water was coming in, and we climbed up on deck. My husband secured one life-belt and placed it around me. We climbed over the rail...but we hung on to the port-hole for a few minutes, and then I heard a slight explosion. Then the water seemed to gush up, and my husband said 'Jump!'...In the water I grasped my husband's clothing and held on to his back; and there we just hung together and swam. My husband swims, but I just kicked and struggled and held on to him, and eventually I found my limbs very stiff, so that I had to be helped into the boat. We were put on the Storstad for a time and then on the Lady Evelyn and put into the cabin.

One man who had a broken leg went insane. There was very little screaming, and there was nothing in the way of unseemly struggles."

For some, the final minutes on the sinking ship were as harrowing as those spent in the water. Captain Rufus Spooner of the Salvation Army admitted, "The awful thing was to see the people trying to get up the staircase. The ship had listed so far over by the time we got up that to try to get upstairs was almost impossible. We got up a few steps, only to fall back again. All round me were frantic men and women, and then, before I could fairly realize where I was or what I could do next, I seemed to be lifted right up and carried forward off the ship into the water."

Despite such testimonials, the water was certainly still more dangerous than the deck of a ship, even one that was sinking, and Spooner's experience in the water was nothing short of terrifying: "I was rolled over and over, twisted round and round, banged against bits of wreckage and got my foot caught in something of iron and rope. I thought I was gone then, for I'm not a great swimmer; but I managed to get free. I swam round till someone got me by the neck and I felt my head going under. I thought again I was gone for certain; but I got free the second time and started out again to try for a boat. It was a narrow shave…The third time, I had sense enough not to spend the little strength I had left, and I got hold of a spar and rolled over on it to keep myself up. I drifted like that for a long time till I was picked up and taken to Rimouski. All I've got left is my bunch of keys, which stuck in my pocket."

The Salvation Army band had been playing when the *Empress* left Quebec, and there were a number of band members on board, among them a J. Johnson, who managed to survive his ordeal, albeit with barely even the clothes on his back. He explained, "We were all asleep in the second cabin when the crash came. I went upstairs to see what had happened and the other three fellows in the cabin stayed behind. Two of them were drowned and one got out. … I saw the people struggling along the corridors to get on deck, but it was awkward because the water was coming into the vessel. Commissioner Rees and some others were just going along in front of me and I assisted them up as well as I could, and eventually we got to the deck, where I lost sight of them."

Seeing that there would be no time to launch the life boats properly, the crew was already cutting them away, allowing each person to take his or her chances in catching one. Johnson explained, "as one went loose I jumped over and hung on to the side, and then got in. I hardly thought they would let me in at first, there were so many in it already. But everyone was helpful. The desire to save themselves did not prevent the occupants of the boat from reaching out a helping hand to others." Though they had made it into a boat, Johnson and his companions were far from safe, and he added, "When I did get in all the ropes were not quite cut, and the liner as nearly on top of us. We seemed to be getting underneath the davits again, and expected every moment to go under. We managed to get away just in time, just as she was sinking, and we were only ten feet away from the steamer when she turned over and went under." Unlike what had been rumored before and since about what happens when large ships sink, Johnson insisted that the final plunge did not create suction as much as it did a wave. When this subsided, he and the others were able to make their way to the *Storstad*.

While most of those who survived did so by depending on their own wits, a few benefited from the kindness of others. One woman recalled, "I and my daughter were helped to the side of the ship by Bandsman Kenneth McIntyre, of the Salvation Army. We crawled to the side and as the ship leaned over we slid over the edge of the deck into the water. Oh, it was cold. I began to be numbed and lost track of my daughter, of whom I have heard no news since…I don't know how long I was in the water; it was so cold, I had almost given up hope, when I seemed to feel arms lifting me out. Then it seemed to get colder than ever for a moment, and the next thing I remember I was on the collier with a crowd of other draggled individuals. From then on, everything was done for me, and even during the train journey up I managed to get rested up a little."

Similarly, as so often happens during a maritime disaster, many of the crewmen ended up saving a countless number of lives. Staff Captain D. McAmmond related one such anecdote: "As the Empress went down, I clung to the taffrail and hung over the vessel's stern. As she sank, I was dragged down into the water, but was immediately forced up again. Down I went again; again, I came up. Finally I managed to swim clear and succeeded in reaching an overturned life-boat. There were several such. A man was already clinging to the boat and he helped me to get a firm hold. We floated along with the boat until we reached another. Holding to this we found a member of the crew. It was a collapsible boat and under his instruction we were able to get it righted and use the oars. It was terribly cold in the water. Some of the people we assisted were so numbed that it was only with the greatest difficulty we succeeded in saving them."

There were a number of heroes that night, but there was perhaps no one as highly praised as Dr. James F. Grant, the ship's physician. Grace Kohl told a reporter, "You must say something very, very nice about Dr. Grant. He was quite wonderful. The way he took charge of things on the Storstad and controlled the situation was marvelous. I think he deserved the thanks of every one, and there is no doubt but that for his skill and quickness in tending people, many more would have died."

Of course, Grant had his own harrowing story of survival. When he ended up in the water, Grant "swam towards the lights of the steamer Storstad, and when nearly exhausted from the struggle and the exposure I was picked up by a life-boat, which went on to the scene of the disaster, and was loaded with survivors, who were pulled out of the water and taken on board the Storstad. Then we were heated and wrapped in blankets, and I was provided with the clothes which I now wear, and which enabled me to do what I could to help the other survivors."

Rather than draw attention to his own efforts, Grant praised the others who served around him, saying, "There was no disorder among the crowd. The captain and other officers remained on the bridge until the vessel sank. ... The life-boats of the Storstad were launched and came rapidly to the rescue. One went back that was not well loaded. About five of the Empress' boats got away. ... The survivors were taken on board the Storstad and the Lady Evelyn, which was summoned by wireless. There everything possible was done for them...."

At the same time, like any other physician, Grant remained haunted by the patients he ultimately could not save: "[I]n at least five cases the shock and exposure were too severe. Four women perished after they reached the Storstad. In each case I was called and the unfortunates died before anything could be done. The last spark of energy had been exhausted. One other woman died just as she was being taken ashore."

While it was the crew's duty to assist passengers, the massive tragedy brought out the best in people, and as family members rushed to each other's aid, they revealed the true meaning of love. After his own rescue, John Black told a reporter, "Thank God I saved my wife; for myself I am not anxious...I was asleep in my bunk when I felt the terrible impact of the collision. At first I thought it must be an evil dream and I saw visions of doomsday. But, looking out through the skylight, I saw frantic seamen rushing to the ship's side, sliding down and, as often as not, being dashed head first into the sea. ... In a flash I saw that the thing had happened. Literally tearing my wife from her berth, I dashed onto the deck, and we both slid down the deck and were projected into the water."

At this point, Black found himself fighting not just for his own life but for that of the woman he loved. He continued, "For a moment I saw nothing but dirty gray. I struggled wildly for the surface, and the time seemed like years. As soon as I got to the surface I saw my wife struggling beside me. Right at our side was a deserted life-boat which must have broken from its davits. I managed to push my wife into it, but was unable to follow myself. So I shouted to my wife to sit tight, and that I would swim until I was picked up...I was picked up by one of the boats from the Storstad. I cannot express the joy and relief I felt when I saw my wife half seated, half lying in the boat...We soon were crying in each other's arms. The men of the *Storstad* treated us well...Not long after the rescue we were taken aboard the Government vessel Lady Evelyn. At Rimouski we were treated and helped in every possible way by Mayor Fiset..."

While those in the water struggled to survive, those on shore, many of them also awakened from a sound sleep, were rushing forward to help. One official with Canadian Pacific later reported, "The *Empress of Ireland* passed and landed her pilot here at 1:30 this morning. There was a haze at the time. At 1:50 a.m. I was awakened by an 'S. O. S.' ring on my door bell and, rushing down, was Informed by a Marconi operator that the *Empress of Ireland* was sinking, having been struck by some vessel. In undress I started to help. No other signal could be got from the doomed vessel. She had no time to give another, as she sank ten minutes after being struck."

The official noted that although "Mr. Whiteside, manager of the Marconi station, rendered effective service by notifying the government steamer Eureka, at Father Point wharf, and the Lady Evelyn at Ramouski wharf," there was little anyone could do. As he explained, "Capt. J. B. Belanger of the Eureka immediately rushed to the scene and Captain Pouliot, with the Lady Evelyn, followed later, his ship being three miles farther away. Meanwhile daylight broke and scanning the horizon with a telescope I saw the two government steamers, nine lifeboats and a collier in the vicinity, going here and there."

While crewmen like Grant were saved and in turn were able to save others, some on board that night made the ultimate sacrifice. One of these men was Sir Henry Seton-Karr, a famous English hunter, author and politician who had served in the House of Commons for over two decades. According to passenger M.D.A. Darling, "My cabin was opposite Sir Henry's, and when I opened my door he opened his, and we bumped into each other in the passageway. He had a life-belt in his hand and I was empty-handed. Sir Henry offered me the life-belt and I refused it. He said, 'Go on, man, take it or I will try to get another man.' I told him to rush out himself and save his own life while I looked after myself. Sir Henry then got angry and actually forced the life-belt over me...Then he pushed me along the corridor. I never saw him after that. He went back to his cabin, and I believe he never came out again, because the ship disappeared a few minutes later. I owe the fact that I am alive to Sir Henry, and, while I believe he lost his life because he wanted to give me the life-belt, I am certain that he would have given it to someone else."

Seton-Karr

Actor Laurence Irving gave his life for that of his wife, actress Mabel Lucy Hackney. F. E. Abbott, a passenger from Toronto, later explained, "I met him first in the passageway, and he said calmly, 'Is the boat going down?' I said that it looked like it. 'Dearie,' Irving then said to his wife, 'hurry, there is no time to lose.' Mrs. Irving began to cry, and, as the actor reached for a life-belt, the boat suddenly lurched forward and he was thrown against the door of his cabin. His face was bloody and Mrs. Irving became frantic. 'Keep cool,' he warned her, but she persisted in holding her arms around him. He forced the life-belt over her and pushed her out of the door. He then practically carried her upstairs."

When Abbott offered to help them, Irving replied, "Look after yourself first, old man, but God bless you all the same." Looking back as he prepared to leave the ship, the last thing Abbott saw of the two was that they were clutched in each other's arms. Other accounts claimed that Irving made it to safety, only to drown in a subsequent attempt to save his wife because she could not swim. Whatever the case, both drowned, and their bodies were never found.

Irving

Hackney

The couple

While some struggled to save their loved ones, others reached out to those they barely knew but still felt a responsibility for. Charles Spencer was a bell-boy on the ship, and he told his unique story: "When the crash came I ran down to the steerage to wake up the boys there and get them to go to the bulkheads and turn them. They are closed by hand wheels. I did not have much time, because when I reached there the water was two feet deep and I could hardly get through it. I know two of the boys were drowned there. I and another, Samuel Baker, were the only bell-boys saved out of the dozen on the vessel...When I woke the boys below I ran to the boat deck where the men were trying to put the life-boats overboard. The Empress had a list to starboard and the top deck was down to the water. She was going very fast. One of the funnels toppled into the water and almost fell on a life-boat. When the boat made a final lurch I dived into the water, because I felt I could get somewhere...When I came up Captain Kendall was near me. He caught hold of me and helped me along, and we were in the water about twenty minutes when we were picked up and taken to the coal boat."

Other officers also perished while doing their duty, including the chief officer. One survivor said of him, "There are few people who really know how the chief officer, Mr. Steede, died. He was at his post to the last and was killed by tumbling wreckage. Each man has his post at a certain boat, and his was at boat No. 8, on the port side. The ship was struck on the starboard, but an effort was made to launch the port side boats at once after the collision. But the list on the vessel made it impossible to get away these boats...We went over to the port side. 'No good, boys, on this side,' said he. 'Go to the starboard.' we went there, but the chief officer remained at No. 8, directing passengers, until he was swept from his post either by falling ropes, boxes or perhaps a boat, for the starboard boats broke loose and did a lot of damage to life. No one actually saw Steede disappear."

One of the most moving tales of the disaster came from Robert W. Crellin, of British Columbia. A wealthy farmer, he saved Florence Barbour, one of only three little girls to survive the ordeal, yet he praised her valor over his own: "The child was pluckier than a stout man. She never even whimpered, and complaint was out of the question. You should have seen how the girls and women in the little village of Rimouski hugged her when we got ashore. Time and time again I feared Florence would lose her hold, and I would speak to her when my mouth and eyes were clear. Each time her little hands would clutch me tighter, until it seemed she'd stop my breath, but I welcomed the hold because it showed she had the pluck and courage needed."

As fate would have it, surviving the wreck was only the beginning of more troubles for Florence. Crellin explained, "Poor child! She lost her mother and sister, and only a year ago her father, William Barbour, of Silverstone, was killed. She's alone in the world, but Florence will never need a friend or home while I have breath in my body."

Ensign E. Pugmire of the Salvation Army shared with his friends a tragic tale of the loss of some of their comrades: "I never got back to my cabin. The life-belts were all there. The ship was already listing over dangerously. ...when I looked over my shoulder as I grabbed the rail, I could see the gangways jammed with people. I passed Major Simcoe's berth going up and asked her if she was not coming. She told me to leave her and find out what the matter was. Her body was among the first picked up on shore." Likewise, "I saw Commissioner Rees when he ran back to get his wife. Major Frank Morris tried hard to save him, for he carried him on his shoulders as long as he could. Morris was a hero. There was an explosion just as the ship went down, and that must have killed hundreds outright. The shock of it blew Morris right overboard. Morris' arm was badly scalded with the steam." He then concluded, "We saw the ship heeling over when we were in the water, but there was no outcry until she had disappeared. The swimmers then shouted to attract the life-boat that was already coming. My comrades died like Salvationists."

As time passed, stories began to emerge about various shortages on the doomed ship that may have cost some people their lives. For example, passenger Lional Kent claimed, "When the boat commenced to slide over I looked for a life-preserver, but found that someone had taken every one of them from the promenade deck. So I went back to my cabin and took the life-preserver on the top of the wardrobe. The majority of passengers did not seem to know that there were life-preservers in their cabins, and although they were easily accessible they were not conspicuous and many could not find them in the confusion, although they looked...The boats on the port side of the liner could not be launched because, owing to the list of the ship, they swung inwards on the davits instead of out over the sea. The only boats that could be launched were those on the starboard side. I think a good many people were injured by the sliding of the port life-boat when it was released, for it slid along the deck to the starboard side and crushed many people against the railings...I think they did marvelously well considering the short time they had to work in. They could not get a foothold on the sloping deck, and there was very little confusion under the circumstances."

Despite the disaster and some of the potential problems that endangered everyone aboard, some passengers, perhaps thoroughly cultivated in the famed British "stiff upper lip" tradition, refused to make much of their experience. J.F. Dutton, originally from London, reported, "The signals woke me up and I lay in my berth amidships on the starboard side. That was the side the collier ran into us, but she was a low boat, and so my cabin was not crushed in as were some of those immediately below me. Directly the collision occurred the Empress began to list, and I immediately went on deck. ... we simply stood there, we knew we were going down, there was no question about that from the first, and it was no good struggling." He then added ruefully, "The poor women were hysterical, but there was no chance to do anything for them. ... As the boat went over we climbed over the rail and slid down the stanchions onto the plates, and walked into the sea. ...I struck out for the rescuing steamer, which was standing about half a mile off. Somehow or another the life-boats appeared and began picking us up."

Once they were in the lifeboats, it was only a matter of time until the survivors reached shore. Dutton concluded, "I was in the water a jolly long time: it seemed like an hour and I believe it was an hour. It was terribly cold and I am stiff all over this morning. I eventually got into a life-boat and was taken on board the collier. They told me there were fifty-three on the life-boat it was quite full up. Dr. Grant was on the collier, and he patched us up until the Lady Evelyn took us ashore."

For his part, Logan Marshall summed up the sentiments of many when he wrote of the death toll as being all but inevitable: "The horrible fact, about which there can be no dispute, is that the Storstad crashed bow on into the side of the big Canadian liner, striking it on the starboard side about mid-way of its length. The steel-sheathed bow of the collier cut through the plates and shell of the Empress and penetrated the hull for a distance of about twelve feet, according to the best testimony. The water didn't flow in. It rushed in. From such stories as could be gathered from survivors and from members of the crew, it appears that Captain Kendall and his officers did all that was humanly possible in the fourteen minutes that the Empress hung on the river."

Recriminations

A picture of coffins being unloaded after the disaster

"Excitement over the cause of the disaster ran high, stimulated by the more or less conflicting stories. Captain Kendall and Captain Anderson, in their public statements, agreed that fog signals were exchanged when their vessels were a considerable distance apart, but there were irreconcilable statements as to the speed and as to the Storstad's conduct immediately after the collision." – Logan Marshall

It took no time at all for news of the accident to spread, and for people to begin to demand details. Sir Thomas Shaughnessy, then president of the Canadian Pacific Railway, issued his first announcement at dawn: "The catastrophe because of the great loss of life is the most serious in the history of the St. Lawrence route. Owing to the distance to the nearest telegraph or telephone station from the scene of the wreck there is unavoidable delay in obtaining official details...From the facts as we have them, it is apparent that about two o'clock this morning the *Empress of Ireland* when off Rimouskl and stopped in a dense fog was rammed by the Norwegian collier Storstad in such a manner as to tear the ship from the middle to the screw, thus making the water-tight bulkheads with which she was provided useless. The vessel settled down in fourteen minutes."

Shaughnessy

Family members began to gather together to await news, and at the Salvation Army Temple, a large crowd of friends and family members of those on board clung to each other and prayed for a miracle. Colonel Rees described the scene and the feeling: "This suspense is the worst of all. We can only wait and pray till the news comes." Likewise, Major McGillivray explained, "It is terrible; we are almost driven distracted. It does not seem possible that it can be true. All our best men in the Dominion were on board that vessel, and it does not seem possible that they can be drowned."

Obviously, the timing of the crash accounted for much of the loss of life. As Shaughnessy pointed out, "The accident occurred at a tune when the passengers were in bed and the interval before the steamship went down was not sufficient to enable the officers to rouse the passengers and get them into the boats, of which there were sufficient to accommodate a very much larger number of people than those on board, including passengers and crew...That such an accident should be possible in the river St. Lawrence to a vessel of the class of the *Empress of Ireland* and with every possible precaution taken by the owners to insure the safety of the passengers and the vessel is deplorable. The saddest feature of the disaster is, of course, the great loss of life, and the heartfelt sympathy of everybody connected with the company goes out to the relatives and friends of all those who met death on the ill-fated steamship."

As word began to get out, papers around the world carried stories. From Montreal came the touching tale of the last moments of men and women who had dedicated their lives to helping others: "When the liner *Empress of Ireland* steamed away from here Thursday, she carried 165 members of the Salvation Army from the United States and Canada, bound for the world convention in London. To the accompaniment of the army band, they were singing, "God Be With You Till we Meet Again." This prelude to the accident in the St. Lawrence made the disaster a near parallel to the sinking of the Titanic, whose passengers sang "Nearer, My God to Thee." as the White Star liner went down."

Then there was this simple obituary from New York: "Laurence S. B. Irving, drowned on steamship *Empress of Ireland*, is an actor, author and manager. He received his education at Marlborough College, College Rollin, Paris, and spent three years in Russia studying for foreign office. His plays are widely known. In 1908 and 1909 he presented sketches of his own authorship in England and America. On May 3, 1910. Mr. Irving addressed the Equal Suffrage league at New York."

As word reached the families of those who were lost, so did the stories of their misery. Again and again, comparisons to the earlier tragedy of the Titanic were made, made all the more fitting since the ship was on its way to England. One report from Liverpool told readers, "Pathetic scenes were, enacted at the office of the Canadian Pacific railway in this city Friday. Crowds of weeping men and women begged for news of the officers and crew of the *Empress of Ireland*, the majority of whom were gathered here. When confirmation of the disaster was received several of the women fainted. Friday's scenes were a duplicate of those witnessed at the time the Titanic went to the bottom."

In the weeks that followed, memorial services were held on both sides of the Atlantic and in many different houses of worship to commemorate the lives lost. Among the most moving eulogies given was one offered by Rabbi Solomon Jacobs, leader of the Holy Blossom Synagogue: "It is with difficulty that I can trust myself to speak on that sad calamity which has touched the heart of Canada and other parts of the civilized world so deeply in the past two days. Ah, it is such blows as these which teach us how fleeting is all human existence, how uncertain the span of life, how our earthly days are measured, our only hope in God. May this sad event remind us of the uncertainty of life and stir us all to a greater sense of our duty to the Great Creator and to each other. Events such as this have a great spiritual purpose to accomplish. They show how weak, how unstable, all our calculations are how man proposes, but God disposes. May the Lord take into His safe-keeping the souls of the departed."

Of course, no religious group suffered as severe a loss as did the members of the Salvation Army. In contemplating the loss of his fellow Commissioner, Commissioner McKie mused, "I should also like to say a few passing words about those whose remains lie in our midst, and to assure the bereaved relatives and friends that the sorrow is international. In the death of Mrs.

Commissioner Rees we have lost a good worker, and the loss is a heavy one. Mrs. Rees was a good mother and helpmeet to her husband. I cannot speak of her without making a reference to the Commissioner. Great as is our sorrow at his being called home, and heavy as we will feel his loss, it would be a source of great consolation to us if we but had his remains with us to lay beside those of his brave wife."

Speaking at a service held at the Salvation Army Temple in Toronto on May 31, Colonel Brengle declared, "God, whenever he finds it necessary to speak to his people very loudly through the medium of what men call a great disaster, chooses those best fitted to cope with the temporary pain and sorrow entailed thereby. Though for the time being the way may seem very dark, **we** must trust God to make the purpose plain and look forward to a glorious future of happiness, united once more with our beloved comrades."

Other eulogies were more secular in nature, such as the one Sir Herbert Tree wrote of Laurence Irving: "We actors were proud of Laurence Irving in life and no less proud of him in death. There was always something fateful about his personality, and one feels that his end is in tragic harmony with his being. Irving was an idealist, fearless of standing by his ideals in any company. He was a scholar in knowledge as in expression, and as an actor had already attained to a great height. His work, like the man himself, was always original."

Tree

Meanwhile, many passengers who survived that fateful night now faced a lifetime of trying to make sense of what happened. Bandsman Green explained, "When I last saw my father, he said, 'Well, boy, we are in God's hands'; and I said, 'Yes, father.' In a second I was parted from all forever. They were all standing together, my father and my mother and my sister Jessie…When I was nine years old, in Boston, I was at death's door for months. My father and mother never expected that I could live, but in their prayers they said to God that they were resigned and were willing that His will should be done. If there was something in store for me, they told Him, they hoped that I might be spared. While I was swimming in the water I thought of this again, and I said practically the same thing my father and mother had said…Now that I am here and alive and comparatively well I want to repeat to you my pledge that I will devote myself and my life to God's work. Somehow or other when I was on the ship I didn't pray. I don't know whether I hadn't time or whether I didn't think of it. It's always the other ship that's going down. You never think that the one you're on will sink."

Jack Saxe, Third Officer for the *Starstad*, insisted that he and his men did all they could for those on board the *Empress*: "We thought we were sinking ourselves after the collision, and did not think the other boat was badly damaged, so we got our boats ready to swing out, and then we heard the cries for help, and we launched our boats and rowed to the rescue. Four times the boat I was in charge of went to and from the scene of the disaster and picked up passengers some dead, but many alive…The first boat from the collier got away in two or three minutes, and I headed her for the liner, which was gradually going over to one side. The first trip made I picked up thirty-two people who were struggling in the icy cold water. I brought them back and they were taken to the Storstad. Then I went back again and picked up sixteen more people alive and eight bodies of people who had died from the shock."

Incensed by the blame being placed on his ship for the accident, he proclaimed, "My crew rowed like demons possessed, and after we had put them on board our ship we rowed back again and got some more people and bodies. These we took to the pilot ship…. The third time we went back the liner was just going under…and when she had disappeared we rowed over the spot and got some of those who were floating about. Their cries for help were awful, but they lasted only a few minutes and then all was silent as the grave."

As Saxe's account indicates, it took no time at all for angry relatives and officials to demand answers. On May 30, a story came from London announcing, "The London morning papers in commenting editorially on the disaster call for a thorough investigation as to whether the bulkheads were closed, and, if so, how was it that the most modern system of watertight compartments failed to keep the ship from sinking?" After all, people had again and again been told that, had the mighty Titanic's bulkhead doors been high enough and closed quickly enough, that ship might have floated long enough for her passengers to be rescued.

Bulkheads were considered the ultimate line of defense against sinking, so it was hard for the public to understand how a ship could sink so fast that there was no time to close them. On the afternoon following the accident, the Prime Minister of Canada, Robert Borden, rose before the Canadian Parliament and told lawmakers, "I would like to say just a word respecting the disaster, tidings of which have been brought to us today in awful suddenness, and in a dreadful toll of human lives taken. The disaster is one which brings a shock such as we in this country have never felt before. I am speaking of the earlier reports. Later reports are more reassuring. I sincerely hope they are true…That this ship, only a few hours out from Quebec, in the dead of night, and with 1,400 passengers on board, should be so badly damaged as to sink in ten or twenty minutes comes to us in this county and this House as a most appalling shock. I do not believe, from reports which have come in, that this is a disaster which could have been averted by anything the country could have done in rendering the navigation of the St. Lawrence more safe…It came in a fog, and could not have been prevented by any safeguards to navigation. In view of the magnitude of the disaster it is fitting that something should be said in this House; that we should express our deepest regret for the disaster and our profound sympathy for those bereaved."

Borden

Sir Wilfrid Laurier, the former prime minister who Borden had replaced just a few years earlier, also weighed in on the issue: "The hand of fate has been heavy against us during the past few months. This is the third disaster on the St. Lawrence route since navigation opened two months ago, and in loss of life it has surpassed anything since the wreck of the Titanic. ... It is premature to express an opinion on the disaster, but it is difficult to believe that such an accident could take place in the St. Lawrence so near to Father Point and not be prevented."

In spite of the acerbic nature of his words, Laurier asserted, "I will not pass judgment, and I hope it will turn out to be one of those disasters which could not have been prevented by human agency. The sympathies of all will go out to the victims, and perhaps in a more substantial way later on. I will join with the Premier in extending to the families of those who have been lost our sincerest and deepest sympathy."

Laurier

At the same time, there was a bigger question, namely over what could have been done to prevent the tragedy. "The [London] Times, in an editorial, considers that nothing could have saved the *Empress of Ireland*, considering the nature of the collision, but asks: 'What was the Storstad doing to run into the *Empress of Ireland* with such suddenness and violence?'" That would prove to be the most controversial issue in the coming investigation.

It seemed from the beginning that the *Storstad* was at fault for the collision, and that her captain's carelessness caused the accident that took so many lives. In the weeks and months that followed, many of that ship's crew members were questioned about the final moments leading up to the crash. One man, who managed to remain anonymous, participated in the following exchange:

Question: "How long before you struck was the signal given to go astern?"

Answer: "It is impossible to say definitely, but it was about a minute; I should say a little longer than a minute.

Question: Are you positive that you got the signal to go at full speed astern?"

Answer: "I am certain the engines were going full speed astern when the collision occurred."

Another crewman reported that, because the *Storstad* was going so slowly in the fog, "The shock of the impact was not very noticeable. I did notice, however, that the engines had been reversed, and we were going full speed astern. That was about one minute before the shock came." Obviously, this was too little too late.

Once the accident occurred, the *Storstad's* crewmen wasted no time jumping into action to rescue those thrown into the water. One officer testified, "It was no trouble to get a boat-load of them. Altogether some sixty were saved on the first trip. So heavily was the boat loaded she all but sank on her return to the <u>Storstad</u>."

Some of the most interesting testimony to come from the people aboard the *Storstad* came not from any member of the crew but from the captain's wife. Mrs. Anderson recalled being summoned from her bed by her husband just moments before the crash. "I ran up to the bridge where Captain Anderson was. Everything was dark and quiet. There was no excitement among the crew and I was cool. 'Are we going to sink?' 'I think so,' he answered. I couldn't cry, although I felt like it. I said to myself, 'My place is here and I will die with my husband.'...Captain Anderson told me he was trying to keep the Storstad in the hole and that if the other liner had not been speeding they would have stopped together for a time at least. My husband ordered two of the officers to go to the bow and see if there was any water pouring in. Again I asked him if we were going down and he answered, 'I can't tell yet.' He said he thought the Empress was all right...I think it was five minutes later that I heard screams and cries, and I shouted to my husband, 'Oh, they are calling.' At first it seemed as if the cries were coming from shore. The captain gave orders to go in that direction and proceeded very slowly. Everywhere around me now I could hear screams. My husband gave orders to send out all the life-boats, and that could not have been ten minutes after the vessels had collided."

It fell to Mrs. Anderson to lead the efforts to revive those pulled from the freezing water. She concluded, "I gave all I had to the passengers and have only what I am standing up in. My husband gave two suits and other clothes away." She also ordered that they be given warm drinks and alcohol for shock.

Little time passed before the British government ordered a Commission of Inquiry to look into the incident, which evoked strong feelings among many. For example, the legendary author Joseph Conrad asserted that there was nothing insidious to be learned from an investigation, writing, "That statesman...does not seem to know that a British Court of Marine Inquiry, ordinary or extraordinary, is not a contrivance for catching scapegoats. I, who have been seaman, mate and master for twenty years, holding my certificate under the Board of Trade, may safely say that none of us ever felt in danger of unfair treatment from a Court of Inquiry. It is a perfectly impartial tribunal which has never punished seamen for the faults of ship owners -- as, indeed, it could not do even if it wanted to... The good ship that is gone... had not been ushered in with beat of drum as the chief wonder of the world of waters. The company who owned her had no agents, authorised or unauthorised, giving boastful interviews about her unsinkability to newspaper reporters ready to swallow any sort of trade statement if only sensational enough for their readers -- readers as ignorant as themselves of the nature of all things outside the commonest experience of the man in the street... The company was content to have as fine, staunch, seaworthy a ship as the technical knowledge of that time could make her. In fact, she was as safe a ship as nine hundred and ninety-nine ships out of any thousand now afloat upon the sea. No; whatever sorrow one can feel, one does not feel indignation. This was not an accident of a very boastful marine transportation; this was a real casualty of the sea."

Conrad

Authors' opinions aside, the commission began its investigation on June 16, 1914. Led by Lord Mersey, who had led the investigation into the *Titanic*'s loss, it met for 11 days and sought to answer 20 questions, including ones such as, "Was *Empress of Ireland* sufficiently and efficiently officered and manned?" and "Was the loss of the Empress or the loss of life, caused by the wrongful act or default of the Master and First Officer of that vessel, and the Master, First, Second and Third Officers of Storstad, or any of them?"

Lord Mersey

A picture of the inquiry in Quebec

Altogether, the commission heard from more than 60 witnesses, most of them members of the crew of either the *Empress of Ireland* or the *Storstad*. Both the ship's captains testified, and naturally, as noted earlier, each defended his actions.

Among the officers testifying in the investigation were a number from the *Storstad*, including one who defended the actions of the Norwegian ship's crew: "Being awakened by a terrible shock, I jumped up immediately and ran out on deck, where I heard the engines going full speed astern. I am a strong man, and have had many experiences during nearly thirty years at sea, but what I saw and heard there made me weep. I still see all those men and women shrieking and struggling in the water. The statement that nothing was done to pick up the survivors is absolutely false; we lowered the boats and rescued over three hundred of those on board the Empress...There was not an officer or a man aboard the *Storstad* who did not do his utmost to save life and comfort the rescued; every man on the ship gave away everything he had. We split up the table-cloths, blankets, etc., to cover the rescued, many of whom were absolutely naked when picked up...Those who had been in the freezing water for an hour or so were at once taken to the engine-room, the warmest place on board, and so numb were they that several sat on the cylinders of the engines, their flesh searing on the hot steel. I am absolutely confident that public opinion will be entirely reversed when the true facts of the case are published."

Only a few passengers were called upon to testify in the investigation. One of them, James Rankin, told the investigators, "I was aroused by the noise and ran out. There was a big pitch to the deck. I really cannot tell you how the accident occurred. I heard the whistle blow when I reached the deck. There was a heavy fog and you could hardly see fifty yards. Five minutes after the collision the fog lifted. The boats on the lower side were in the water and four or five of them got away and saved many people." He went on to speculate, "I think that if the collier had kept her bow in the hole she had made in the Ireland's side, she would have been able to make the shore and probably have saved every one. The behavior of the officers on the Empress was beyond all praise. They did everything they could. The engineers remained below until they could get no more steam and the lights went out."

A few of the witnesses' testimonies came in written form, the result of the witnesses being too injured or ill to appear in court. One these men was Chief Engineer Sampson, whose dedication to his job kept him in the engine room fighting fires until the water finally became so deep that it extinguished them. He wrote, "I was in the engine-room until the lights went out and there was no more steam. I had great difficulty in reaching the decks owing to the great list of the ship. No sooner had I got on deck, when the boats of the port side, which had broken loose, swept down on top of us and carried us under water. When I came to the surface I found myself under a life-boat and entangled in wreckage."

Sampson nearly lost his life then and there, but it was apparently not his time to go. He continued, "I was finally pulled into one of the boats and could see the collier about a mile and a half away. Immediately before the collision we went full speed astern and then stopped. Then I got the order full speed ahead, but had only started the engines when the crash came. We then kept her full speed ahead to try to reach the shore as long as we had steam…Owing to the steam failing us and then the lights also, we could keep the engines going for only a few moments. There was no explosion of any kind. I saw no reason why the collier did not keep much closer than she did, as, if she had, there would have been many lives saved. I am also of the opinion that had she stuck to us we should have reached the shore."

Not every witness called had been on one of the ships that night. William James, a wireless operator at Father Point, was sound asleep when the accident occurred. However, his assistant woke him up just moments after the collision. He took over the wireless at that time, informed two other ships, the *Eureka* and the *Lady Evelyn*, of what had happened, and asked for their help. It took Captain Boulanger of the *Eureka* two passes before he was able to locate the spot of the disaster. By then, all that was left for him to do was to gather bodies.

It was difficult for such men, surrounded by the dead, to avoid pinning the blame on someone or something, and the *Storstad* presented an attractive target, especially since she did not remain attached to the *Empress*. Still, Captain A. J. Elliott, a member of the staff of the Canadian Pacific Railway, conceded, "It has been said that the Storstad backed out of the hole in the Empress' side and did not give her passengers an opportunity to crawl over her sides. That is not true. The Storstad kept her engines ahead after the collision and attempted to keep her nose in the breach of the other's side. It did for a few moments, or may be minutes, but the momentum of the *Empress of Ireland* still carried the greater ship ahead and drew the smaller vessel around with her."

The results, he maintained, were inevitable: "Consequently the lighter vessel was pushed out of the hole and could be of no assistance. As to a difference between signals, those for port and those for starboard are always the same, of course, and would not be misinterpreted if heard. But as to signals for fog and for clear weather, there is a difference. The fog signals are blasts prescribed by law of a duration of not less than three seconds, but they still are different from the port and starboard signals."

Moreover, a number of the passengers who were questioned by the Commissioners insisted that the fog appeared so suddenly that there was little time for the captains of the vessels to react. One testified, "The Empress had been whistling and signaling to a ship ahead. From the signals I thought there must be a vessel approaching us. Then I suddenly realized from my long experience at sea that something was wrong. I looked out and listened to the signals, and it seemed to me that the other vessel was taking a chance of crossing our bow. A moment later I realized that they had lost this chance, and the collier instead of crossing our bow had struck us square amidships."

Pilot Nault chose to focus on the positive outcomes of the tragedy rather than criticize others. "When the survivors of the Empress were brought aboard the Storstad after being picked up in the few boats the collier had aboard, everything possible was done for them. Captain Anderson and his wife surrendered every bit of clothing they possessed to protect the survivors from the cold. They even had to improvise garments. The Storstad steered surprisingly well all the way up the river. With the assistance of the Lord Strathcona we had little difficulty in making eleven or twelve miles an hour...As far as we could ascertain from an examination on board, the ship had some twenty plates sprung forward, but aft of that she is not damaged. After we left Quebec we flooded her aft compartments in order to keep her head up. There is no water in her hold, and she stayed on an even keel throughout the trip. Captain Anderson has taken the tragedy much to heart. Several times on our way up here I have found him crying. He was very much worked up over it, and was very, very sorry."

When asked whether Captain Anderson told him anything regarding how the collision occurred, Nault replied, "No; he would say nothing about it. He said he was under orders not to talk. He told me that he had managed to pick up three hundred and forty of the people from the *Empress*, and had done everything in his power to make them comfortable until they were transferred to the relief steamers."

In the end, the Commissioners decided that the blame must be placed on the *Storstad* since it had changed its course; had it continued in the direction it was originally going, there would have been no accident. The report specifically targeted Chief Officer Toftenes, who ordered the course change, though Anderson stood by his crew, criticizing the report and calling Mersey a "fool."

Interestingly, but perhaps not surprisingly, an inquiry undertaken by officials in Norway drew the opposite conclusion and blamed Kendall for the accident because he did not follow standard procedure and pass the *Storstad* port to port.

Even as blame was being determined and apportioned, there was still the matter of the financial impact of the loss. As the *London Times* article noted, "The claim for the *Empress of Ireland* will be the heaviest suffered by the Lloyds underwriters since the sinking of the Titanic. It is expected that the disaster will give a serious check to the scheme for establishing a Canadian Lloyds, with a view of reducing the rates charged in London for insuring vessels navigating the St. Lawrence. Statistics show that the underwriters have consistently lost money on such voyages, owing to the dangers of the river and the prevalence of fogs and ice."

Indeed, Canadian Pacific Railway would take the owners of the *Storstad*, A.F. Klaveness & Co., to court, and in the end, the court ruled in favor of the plaintiff to the tune of $2,000,000. That figure covered the valuation of silver deposits aboard the *Empress of Ireland*. A.F. Klaveness & Co., in an effort to argue the *Empress of Ireland* was at fault, filed a counterclaim for $50,000 in damages, a claim that the court rejected. As a result of the court actions, the *Storstad* would be seized and sold, with the proceeds going towards the judgment.

Of course, no monetary value could be placed on the lives that were lost that day. 1,012 of the 1,477 people on the ship died, giving the event a death toll rivaling even the Titanic. Almost all the children were lost, with only 4 of the 138 making it safely to land. Nearly 90% of the women also went down with the ship or drowned, and most of the 172 men who made it out alive were members of the crew who were sufficiently familiar with the ship to get off safely. Far from being a damning indictment of their efforts to save passengers, the statistics demonstrate the grim and grisly fact that there was such little time to do anything before the ship was gone.

In the end, Logan Marshall may have put it best when he wrote, "The universal sympathy which is written in every face and heard in every voice proves that man is more than the beasts that perish. It is an evidence of the divine in humanity. Why should we care? There is no reason in the world, unless there is something in us that is different from lime and carbon and phosphorus, something that makes us mortals able to suffer together 'For we have all of us an human heart.'"

A commemorative plaque at Pointe-au-Père

Online Resources

Other books about shipwrecks by Charles River Editors

Other books about famous shipwrecks on Amazon

Bibliography

Conrad, J. (1919) *The Lesson of the Collision. A monograph upon the loss of the "Empress of Ireland."* London: Richard Clay and Sons, Ltd.

Croall, J. (1980) *Fourteen minutes: The last voyage of the Empress of Ireland.* Sphere, London.

Grout, D. (2001) *Empress of Ireland: An Edwardian Liner.* Gloucestershire: Tempus Press.

Grout, D. (2014) *RMS Empress of Ireland. Pride of the Canadian Pacific's Atlantic Fleet.* Gloucestershire: The History Press.

Logan, Marshall. (1914) *The Tragic Story of the Empress of Ireland: an Authentic Account of the Most Horrible Disaster in Canadian History, Constructed From the Real Facts Obtained From Those on Board Who Survived and Other Great Sea Disasters.* Philadelphia: John C. Winston.

Wood, H.P. (1982) *Till we Meet Again: The Sinking of the Empress of Ireland.* Toronto : Image Pub.

Zeni, D. (1998) *Forgotten Empress. The Empress of Ireland Story.* Halsgrove; 1st Canadian edition

Free Books by Charles River Editors

We have brand new titles available for free most days of the week. To see which of our titles are currently free, click on this link.

Discounted Books by Charles River Editors

We have titles at a discount price of just 99 cents everyday. To see which of our titles are currently 99 cents, click on this link.

Made in the USA
Coppell, TX
08 November 2020

40953515R00026